REEL TIME

PUBLISHED BY CREATIVE EDUCATION AND CREATIVE PAPERBACKS
P.O. BOX 227, MANKATO, MINNESOTA 56002
CREATIVE EDUCATION AND CREATIVE PAPERBACKS
ARE IMPRINTS OF THE CREATIVE COMPANY
WWW.THECREATIVECOMPANY.US

DESIGN AND PRODUCTION BY CHRISTINE VANDERBEEK
ART DIRECTION BY RITA MARSHALL
PRINTED IN THE UNITED STATES OF AMERICA

PHOTOGRAPHS BY ALAMY (WALTERFRAME), CORBIS (PHILIP JAMES CORWIN,
DAVE REEDE/ALL CANADA PHOTOS, BRIAN SUMMERS/FIRST LIGHT, YANGZHENG/
CPRESSPHOTO), ISTOCKPHOTO (GIVAGA, IPGGUTENBERGUKLTD, MOLOKO88),
SHUTTERSTOCK (JEFF FEVERSTON, GWB, OLEGDOROSHIN, PINOSUB, ALEXANDER
RATHS, ROCKSWEEPER, STEVENRUSSELLSMITHPHOTOS, EVLAKHOV VALERIY,
VOLOSINA, ZHELTYSHEV), SUPERSTOCK (M. WATSON/ARDEA.COM/PANTHEO/
PANTHEON)

LIBRARY OF CONGRESS CATALOGING-IN-PUBLICATION DATA
ROSEN, MICHAEL J.
THE PERFECT SPOT / MICHAEL J. ROSEN.
P. CM. – (REEL TIME)
INCLUDES INDEX.
SUMMARY: A PRIMER ON THE BASIC DOS AND DON'TS OF FISHING, INCLUDING TIPS
ON FINDING AND ACCESSING NEW FISHING SPOTS, ADVICE ON HOW TO AVOID
POLLUTED WATERS, AND INSTRUCTIONS FOR MAKING A CREEL.

ISBN 978-1-60818-774-4 (HARDCOVER)
ISBN 978-1-62832-382-5 (PBK)
ISBN 978-1-56660-816-9 (EBOOK)
THIS TITLE HAS BEEN SUBMITTED FOR CIP PROCESSING UNDER LCCN 2016010301.

CCSS: RI.3.1, 2, 3, 4, 5, 7, 8, 10; RI.4.1, 2, 3, 4, 7, 10; RI.5.1, 2, 4, 10;
RF.3.3, 4; RF.4.3, 4; RF.5.3, 4

FIRST EDITION HC 9 8 7 6 5 4 3 2 1
FIRST EDITION PBK 9 8 7 6 5 4 3 2 1

THE PERFECT SPOT

→ MICHAEL J. ROSEN ←

CREATIVE EDUCATION ⚓ CREATIVE PAPERBACKS

TABLE OF CONTENTS

WELCOME TO THE CLUB

W henever you drop your hook into the water, you add a "line" to the long story of fishing. People have been fishing for thousands of years. There have been a few changes: Gear that was once handmade can now be bought. Boats are now powered by engines. Anglers can travel faster and farther out to sea. But otherwise, fishing has changed very little. It is pretty much the same today as it was for the first people who put a worm on a hook.

Nor have the fish changed much. Today's fish are much like those that lived thousands of years ago. And the fish closest to you are much like the fish thousands of miles away.

Fishing is a sport you can "win" by enjoying it. As an angler, you fish for the day, the weather, and the scenery. But most of all, you fish for the challenge. Did you cast your bait in the right spot? Did you attract a fish with your lure? Release it unharmed? Then you have won!

So, welcome to the oldest unofficial club on Earth. Anglers of all ages are invited. All that is required to join is a promise: Follow all the rules, respect other anglers and the environment, and be safe.

Some hooked fish leap out of the water as they fight to get free.

WATER WORLD

Salmon swim to clear, shallow waters to lay their eggs.

The first anglers knew very little about the watery world of fish. Though many years have passed, what an angler knows hasn't changed much. You still drop a line into the water. You still struggle with a different intelligence (fish) under the surface. But today, there is sadly less clean water in which fish can live.

Fish are sensitive to changes in their surroundings. Fish cannot stay cool in water that is too shallow. They need places to hide so that they can safely lay eggs. Fish need plenty of oxygen to be able to breathe. If there are too many of one kind of fish or too few of another, there

A healthy wetland habitat is good for fish and other life forms.

isn't a healthy balance. Any one of these problems can lead to many others.

Fish can be found under the frozen waters of Earth's poles. They can be seen in the steamy swamps of the tropics. Fish swim in icy currents racing down mountains. They glide through the deep trenches of the oceans. People want to catch fish in each of these places.

People aren't the only ones who enjoy freshly caught fish!

THE PERFECT SPOT → CHAPTER 3

FINDING YOUR SPOT

Do your research on a new spot to find out which gear you'll need to land a fish.

One fish or another is likely swimming close to where you live. Is there a body of water nearby? Then you already know a spot to try your luck! A map of your area will show other places where you can cast your line.

YOU CAN ALSO FIND GOOD FISHING SPOTS IF YOU ...

- Talk to other anglers. Ask where they like to fish. Talk to people who work at tackle shops, too.

- Check out fishing magazines and local newspapers. They may list places near you. Some might even have helpful fishing tips.

- Call your state's agency that manages fish and wildlife resources. Or visit their website. Search for state parks online, too. Most will have a fishing area.

- Look into local fishing groups. Summer camps, scouting clubs, and recreation centers often have events and programs for anglers.

- Search for bodies of water on private properties. Be sure to get permission first.

Check out a local business, housing complex, office park, or golf course. Many will have a pond or stream.

- ■ **Approach the owner of a pond.** Some people stock their ponds with fish to limit plant and **algae** growth. Always ask permission before fishing on private land. Respect the owner's property. Observe whatever limits they set.

- ■ **Talk to the owner of a waterfront property.** They don't own the water or the fish, but they do own the land. Ask if you can walk across their land to get to the water.

- ■ **Seek out pay ponds.** These are filled with certain kinds of fish. Pay ponds are good for practice. But you do lose the challenge of finding and outsmarting a fish. You also miss out on the peace and quiet of nature.

THE PERFECT SPOT ⟶ CHAPTER 4

LOOK FOR THE SIGNS

Fish cannot survive in water choked by too much algae growth.

Many bodies of water are in danger. Litter, dumping of wastes, and harmful runoff pollute water. Some places you might like to try fishing could be dirty. The fish might not be safe to eat— *if* fish still swim there.

LEARN TO RECOGNIZE POLLUTED WATER. DON'T FISH WHERE THE WATER IS:

- **Very green.** When too much algae grow, the water thickens. It becomes dark and cloudy. It is not safe for plants and animals to live there.

- **Cloudy or muddy.** Fish can't breathe if too much dirt is mixed up in the water. In healthy water, plant life helps keep the dirt settled.

- **Shiny with a film, frothy, or clotted with scum.** These can be signs of leaking sewage or oil.

- **Covered with an orange or red layer.** This suggests that chemicals have seeped into the water.

- **Smelling like rotten eggs.** Aside from being unpleasant, that smell could signal leaking sewage.

Frogs enjoy clean water.

Instead, look for a place that is full of life. A bank with healthy green plants. Clear water where you can see minnows and plants below. Splashes made by leaping frogs and jumping fish. This is the perfect spot to cast your line.

ACTIVITY: A COOL CREEL

❧

A CREEL IS A LIGHTWEIGHT CARRIER FOR YOUR
CATCH. MANY ANGLERS USE A COOLER OR A
BASKET, BUT YOU CAN MAKE YOUR OWN CREEL
TO SLING OVER YOUR SHOULDER.

MATERIALS

- an old pillowcase or cloth sack
- scissors

1 Starting at the open end of the sack, make two cuts, two inches apart. Cut a quarter of the way down the sack. On the other side of the opening, directly across from the first two cuts, make two more cuts, two inches apart.

2 Tie the two-inch bands together to create a strap. The remaining wider flaps can be folded over the day's catch.

3 Add a layer of grass, leaves, or ferns to the bottom of the sack and place a fish on top. Continue to layer plants and fish until you've packed up your catch. Fold the flaps over your load. Soak the sack in water to keep the fish cool and moist.

❧

GLOSSARY

algae → large groups of simple plants that grow in water

anglers → people who fish

cast → the action used to place a baited line out in the water

currents → the directions in which bodies of water are moving

lure → a type of bait someone makes, not a natural one such as a fly, worm, or other animal

trenches → long, deep ditches in the floor of oceans

READ MORE

Bourne, Wade. *The Pocket Fishing Basics Guide: Freshwater Basics, Hook, Line & Sinker*. New York: Skyhorse, 2012.

Levine, Michelle. *Fish*. Mankato, Minn.: Amicus, 2015.

WEBSITES

Idaho Public Television: Fish

http://idahoptv.org/sciencetrek/topics/fish/index.cfm

Watch a fish video, read fish facts, and more!

Take Me Fishing: How to Fish

http://www.takemefishing.org/how-to-fish/

Learn more about fishing, and find places to fish near you!

Note: Every effort has been made to ensure that the websites listed above are suitable for children, that they have educational value, and that they contain no inappropriate material. However, because of the nature of the Internet, it is impossible to guarantee that these sites will remain active indefinitely or that their contents will not be altered.

INDEX